SO-AEJ-662

The
Phoenix Collection
&
Other Poems

The
Phoenix Collection
&
Other Poems

MAX PRESTON

www.ivyhousebooks.com

PUBLISHED BY IVY HOUSE PUBLISHING GROUP
5122 Bur Oak Circle, Raleigh, NC 27612
United States of America
919-782-0281
www.ivyhousebooks.com

ISBN13: 978-1-57197-479-2
Library of Congress Control Number: 2007926142

© 2007 Max Preston
All rights reserved, which includes the right to reproduce this book or
portions thereof in any form whatsoever except as provided by the
U.S. Copyright Law.

Printed in the United States of America

This book of poetry is dedicated to my family and friends—
past and present. I hope that I have no enemies.

TABLE OF CONTENTS

FOREWORD

This, the ides of March, was the very day three years ago when Max Preston stood in our living room in Hillsborough, North Carolina and read his poetry to seventy somewhat-surprised friends and neighbors. We knew Max, or thought we did. We knew him as a lawyer, an historic preservationist, a father, a grandfather, a Texan, a churhgoer, a traveler, a kind friend, and a great dancer. Some knew him as a puppeteer. Some knew of his spiritiual quest, a search for not just answers but for more and more possibilities of this life and beyond. And that March afternoon, in our crowded, standing-room only house, we were introduced to Max Preston, the poet.

I knew the poet. I was honored when Max appeared at the kitchen door one afternoon a few months earlier with a brown kraft envelope full of his work. I skimmed a few poems, asked to keep them for a few days so that I could read and re-read and reflect. In clear, straight-forward language, Max's poetry seems the distillation of a thoughtful life. He writes of the majesty of nature, the quicksilver sense of life's ironies, the spiritual inquiry requisite in unraveling the mysteries of the universe. He explores life cycles, regeneration and transfiguration, the depths of love. The themes are often lofty, and the language accessible, even musical, his verse bearing a cadence and rhythm that draw you in and hold you rapt.

Not bad for a career corporate attorney, not bad at all. Continuing a time-honored tradition of poets toiling away in the not-so-hallowed halls of commerce, Max spent more than three decades working for a telecommunications firm. Max was the attorney and executive; his late wife, Norma, was the artist. Norma's canvasses graced the walls of homes, galleries, museums, while Max, the attorney-cum-poet quietly and diligently pursued his own creative path. Her painting, "Phoenix Bird Rising," which graces the cover of Max's volume of poetry, displays the powerful interconnection of birth and death, triumph and defeat, archetypal themes at work in Max's poems.

On March 15th, a decidedly auspicious day to go public, Max Preston the poet stepped forward. Three years later, Max steps forward again with *The Phoenix Collection and Other Poems.* Unlike the soothsayer's dire warning, though, Max's poems invite us to observe more closely, consider more fully, live more joyfully.

—ELIZABETH WOODMAN
March 15, 2007

ACKNOWLEDGEMENTS

Many thanks are due to those who have shared my readings and even said kind words; but special thanks go to my deceased wife, Norma, and to my present wife, Patricia, for pushing me to publish. Also, special thanks to Kathleen Faherty for reveiwing my poems and making suggestions where she saw the need, and later, made suggestions as to the arrangement of the poems to assist their presentation in book form. Thanks also go to Ann Humphreys, who taught critiquing, and gave personal help and insights on various ways to sort and arrange the poems to enhance their flow in the book. I am very grateful to Elizabeth Woodman for arranging a reading of my poems in her historic home, and indeed, because she kindly agreed to write the foreword for *The Phoenix Collection*. Thanks to the Hillsborough Literary Society for inviting me to read my poetry, along with a gifted poet, Lee Rogers. Lee has befriended me in many ways in the publishing of this book. I say "good work" and "thanks" to the artists, Patricia Merriman, Grant Preston and Abby Preston, for the drawings preceding some of the poems. Much appreciation to Ivy House Publishing Group, publishers of this work, who guide me still.

The painting on the front cover of this book was painted by my deceased wife, Norma. It was on her easel when she died. Although unsigned, I believe it was essentially complete. I call the painting "Phoenix Bird Rising" as that is what it suggests to me. Who can say?

—MAX PRESTON

SECTION I

Little Phoenix

The mountain speaks to me in silence—
the silence of the fog-enshrouded trees;
the box turtles that make no sound;
the spiders that quietly weave their webs,
leaving behind their messages glistening with dew.
Good Friends communicate without words.

Mountain Weaver

The mountain weaver spins her thread;
She builds a web as she is led—
And throws it like a fisher's net
Upon the wind and misty dew—
And waits, in patience, as the trap is set
In beauty to attract the catch—
The spider does what it must do.
The fly, likewise, is made for this.
Its job is done; its time now spent,
Is ready for entanglement.
The weaver weaves; the fly gets caught.
(No guilt is laid; it comes to naught)
The spider, web and fly are one,
The watcher and the watcher's son.

At Meditation Point

I sat along the trail at Meditation Point,
the fate of every person in my thoughts.
Into my consciousness came the tree, which wasn't there,
(a large chestnut that lightning had struck many years before,
lay in decay across the forest floor).
A tiny worm moved across the remnants of the stump
with no regard for time or space,
or even for the thing over which it crawled.
The tree, long lifeless, now without form,
is a portion of the ceaseless symmetry
that produces the new chestnut sprout,
beside the rotting body of the other,
like a child who steps into its dead parent's shoes.

I Sit Within the Stillness of the Woods

I sit within the stillness of the woods;
I am wrapped in its protection.
I am the deer hiding from the hunter;
I am the woodpecker drilling for my food,
diligently pursuing the bug beneath the bark;
I am the box turtles crawling slowly across the forest floor.
My mind is lifted by the winds to Mother Sky;
my ancient instinct is to live, survive.
But, I am not the deer who sometimes hides in fear;
I am not the woodpecker whose food is just beneath the bark;
I left the forest floor a million years ago.
How can I go back?

Storm on Little Phoenix Mountain

The winds precede the ominous clouds
Shaking the trees as if they have been bad children.
Then, there is instant calm.
I stand anticipating the next blow—it comes.
The trees twist and sway like tribal dancers;
Limbs, as arms, wave and gyrate
While the clouds slowly approach;
Then pour out their bounty—purifying the air,
Thundering and electric—
Savage and frightening.
Trees fall—the ritual calling forth sacrifice
To appease the gods—
The awesome power of the storm.

Blue Ridge Uplift

The mountains flow across the landscape
Suggesting the time when they came crashing,
Beating against the new rock shore;
Old, but new, mellowed by passing time;
Beyond facelifts and tummy tucks—
Too old to care.

I Hear the Lion Roar

I hear the lion roar. It waits outside the door to devour me.
Inside I feel safe from the sinister sound.
But how long can I stay within my nice cocoon—
A chrysalis that ignores all around it until the appointed time?
As the wasp is ready, so is the lion.
I will think the lion away: "There is no lion.
The world is a safe place. There are no terrible claws or jaws."
The cold, icy roar brings me back to fear—a fear that does no
     good.
Am I imprisoned by the chilly blast of fear instigated by this or
     that?
The lion is there; the lion is here.
I am here; I am there.
I am the lion; the lion is I.
If I am eaten I will be sustained.
My appointment is not yet;
Not until I sit down to dine with the lion.
And while it has its meal I feel a part of it all;
But not the me that I am, for I am the lion.
The lion has dispatched me and my fears.

Little Phoenix "2"

I see the mountain breathing—
Respiring as surely as any other living thing.
When the air is cold, its breath fogs the valley
And it huddles into itself, shivering to preserve its warmth.
In summer, its cheeks shine with the radiant sun
That wets its shirt with sweat.
Its health is shown by the vigor of its flowers and trees
Which share its soil.
Lady slippers do not look happy with child abuse:
Smooth skin suggests good care.
A bloody cut requires stitches;
A scratch demands a loving kiss.
A pure heart gives up pure water;
A spirit clogged by garbage produces a sickly soul.
The mountain moans its pain and sings its joy.

The Unkindest Cut

The roads ran blood
from gaping wounds.
The brazen killers hacked the body
in plain view.
Still plotting its dismemberment,
they took away her beauty
and left her bare and torn.
The heavens cried and washed away
the sorrowful sight.
   God made a mountain.
   Man dug a hole.

The Spider Pod

The spider pod is beautiful—
probably filled with eggs or little spiders.
It hangs in the small holly bush—
An upside-down hot-air balloon
Hanging by its strings as if the gondola
Was caught in a tree.
Why, that spider is a first class craftsman;
Her pod seems perfect in dimension and symmetry.
Its beige color tinges to copper.
The spider's silk-like threads glisten silver in the sun.
Man, I don't know; I am a male, macho enough,
But that spider built a beautiful thing
And she ought to be recognized for it.

March Snow

March is quixotic, exotic and wet.
Spring has promised and St. Thomased,
But not yet.
The birds are in a quandary—a regular flutter—
A robin flies in—I fear too soon;
The weather still sings a Winter tune.
The weatherman predicts rain, so it snows;
Minute by minute—that's how March goes.

Johnny J

Johnny Jump-up,
Little rover of the garden,
Like a cat with its own mind—
You plant it here; it grows there.
Delicate blossoms, delivered by a tough guy.

My Little Garden

While drinking my coffee this morning,
My spirits rise as I look out from my kitchen window.
My little garden has a glow.
The sun is shining through the hollyhock petals
Making them translucent to the eye.
The flowers are backgrounded by the white picket fence,
Behind which gleams the sunlight on my strawberry patch.
I borrow my distant view from my neighbor's yard.
My heart is a vast estate.

Golden Morning

I am wealthy this morning.
Goldfinches have brought the mother lode to my feeder
And the cost to me is peanuts and thistle seeds.

Fruit Salad on the Mountain

There is fruit salad on the mountains.
Nights are cold; winter is coming.
The leaves must escape;
Under the cover of darkness many go south.
Some take a bolder stance and fall in plain view,
As if to say: "I am protected by my unalienable right to fall."
They strike awe in their viewers by their stunning camoflage
Of lemon-yellow, apple-red, and orange-orange,
With some lettuce-green tossed in.
It makes a beautiful table.

The Hourglass of Seasons

I watched the leaves fall;
They were unnumbered—
Anonymous.
I watched the leaves fall;
They had served their time
Without regret.
I watched the leaves fall;
Majestic in death . . .
Proclaiming winter.

A December Morning

Breathing in and out among the trees,
The fog drifts here and there, as if moved by angels' wings,
Giving a comforting quietness to Little Phoenix this morning.
First it comes in close to say, "Hello,"
Then slips away to hide among the trees to watch.
It caresses the wintry nakedness of the forest silhouettes with a
    soft silence.
There is no world beyond its veil as it controls the universe
In its encasing peace, like love, tender and complete.

A Mountain Christmas

Fierce winds may blow;
Trees struggle to keep their place
Against the ice and rime and snow.
They stand with nature's grace
And say to Man,
"Hold out your hand and do not tire;
Enjoy your place beside the fire
With family all around
And friends nearby to share another year."

The Many Moods of Mona

Today I watch Mona, shrouded in fog.
She is enigmatic, not easy to know,
In early morning quiet—
Before the world declares her a part of commerce—
The impression of a bridge Sissily has painted—
Suggesting something more.
Bridge lights still glow in fuzzied, haloed circles
Dimming as day's light comes.
This morning, the lady is cold, her surface hard;
She hides the warmth and pleasures
That she bestows at other times.
The lady does not want to change so soon.
Trees stand along the shore, vague as distant travelers.
The sun infuses a sky-glow of pink,
As snow-fog slowly turns from gray-white to translucent blue.
Mona's face emerges as if against her will;
The day must come, but she holds back—
Mysterious as a cat that rises quickly to unknown calls—
She will drop her veil as it suits her mood.

Whiteout

Along Lake Michigan's shore on 196
I travel comfortably without concerns
Motoring north in a light snow mix
Seeing the highway and feeling the turns.
Suddenly the snow has become a wall—
No visibility front or back—
A solid blanket like a pall.
I can't see the center or the roadside track.
In daylight hours—completely blind;
I imagine trucks speeding one brake pulse behind.
I have no guidelines on which to bank;
Nothing, really, is in my control—
(I'm drowning in a virtual deprivation tank).
Pulling over to stop would make no sense.
I am near panic—how long can it last?
If I miss a curve I may hit a fence.
I am driving slowly. Is that too fast?
Nothing visible, nothing at all.
Adrift . . . adrift . . . risk everywhere.
A soul cut off from the mercy of God
And to physical senses the door is shut—
A vacuum sucking away my breath.
A person impelled on a suicide path;
I cannot stop; I can't turn aside.
A question within: "Have I already died?"
I can't shake loose from the panic I feel.
My eyes squint; my muscles are tense.
My mind is boxed as I grip the wheel—
A grinding wheel—miles grinding against time;
It's grinding me down until I don't exist.
Sucked into the great maw of the snowstorm,

Will I ever come out—or be spit up dead?
I am floating . . . falling into a well.
The white, white, white . . . miles of white road ahead
What! What's up ahead?
A Golden Arch—a Big Mac for sale!
I park; I sag; I sigh welcome relief;
The McDonald's sign has broken the spell.
Survived the whiteout, I've conquered the beast.
I laugh inside; then I laugh out loud.
I sit there and laugh at the ironic twist—
The storm spit me up like a Jonah of old,
Testing my limits, it brought me to this—
A roadside Nineveh—but the coffee is cold.

SECTION II

The Cycle of Man

The cycle of Man is strange indeed.
The ball of twine is found unwound;
Then wound back up until its time,
To toss away again.

Ah! Romance

A Deeper Love

Love's light is short unless supported by a deeper love
That overlooks the human faults that lie beneath the night,
Looming large when daylight comes,
But when perceived as friends they balance off like left and right.

I Love, But Do Not Speak

Can't you hear words that are not spoken—
My thoughts, which from fear I cannot say.
Ovid expresses these in greater token;
Unpolished words might frighten you away.
   I talk of Presidents and Kings—
    Of politics and material things—
   Because I am not certain.

The poets speak as I cannot,
And under critics they have passed the test.
My feelings tangle in an unversed plot,
Are lost like twigs within a sparrow's nest.
   I race into philosophic thought,
    Fearing emotions, as Daphne, might be caught—
   Because I am not certain.

Instead Let's Kill The Lioness

Where is the fissure in the wall—
Must words on barren rock descend?
When I lift my voice to call,
The lack of outlet makes it bend.
Is there no way to reach you
Behind the silent brick;
Is there no magic, no fantasy, nor trick
To make this barrier vanish?
    Try it—find the niche.

Your Whispered "Yes"

When the tortured soul in silence has kept quiet,
Only letting words live in the eyes;
The ship of soul sits listing in the night—
Marooned until the high tides rise.
Nor can this ship be satisfied with any cargo,
Nor cargo gained at many different ports;
And, while impounded by its own embargo,
It creaks to reach the object that it courts.
Looking just this far and no further—
Ensnared by a sweetly woven rope—
Desiring this one thing, and no other,
To quicken life in hopeless hope.
    Yet, in hoping to be lifted from this sea,
    Your whispered "yes" is its sole charity.

Illa Femina Pulchra

This it is, the tear-shaped droplet,
Reaping radiance like a prism
Making known to all around it,
Without boasting, "I am beauty."
Bitter would other sweetness tend
Beside this sapid visual feast,
Wafting up on wings of wind
To revive and drive the thirst-crazed beast.
Flood me with your flashing frailty
Into my cardial cup;
Wasting not a drop of beauty,
I will live and sup.

Little Bird

Little bird, I will give you energy to fly;
I am the sky.
I will be your sun when you are cold.
If you are bold,
I will lift you in my arms—
  (My hands are warm);
But you are free to fly away—
Or stay with me.
My arms are open—
Open as the sky.

The Woman

The bubbling of a clear stream
The music of a breeze in trees
The little Rufous hummingbird
The fluffy feathers and delicate size
The movement of the cat
Sleek, lithe, natural elegance
The womanliness, the woman, wanting
The eyes, the look, the high luster
The rise of radiance—a sweet blush
The softening skin—the touch, the touch.
      The Woman.

The Wedding

Seizing the time from a closing flower,
The bee frantically processes the last nectar
For the long winter
While the trees play dress-up—
Decked out in passing splendor—
Then cast down their clothes like scolded children.
The seconds, the minutes, the hours, the days, the weeks,
The months, the seasons, the years—
The wedding—the beautiful white light, the radiant light,
The energy of light—full of energy.
The wedding guests, from a hundred separate lives
Of countless passing joys and sorrows of connected acts,
Come together as if hoping to call back the rush of time.
And there the two (today the aura of green and white)
To risk the uncertain.
If loving, if caring, if consideration—
Then the uncertain,
With trees and rocks and hills and wind and hail,
May become a certain memory
That prompts the sweet tear or unbid sigh.
Every year the bee comes; every year the seasons;
Whether the same bee or season, there is connectivity.
And the first pulls the next forward;
And the baby cries and laughs
And pulls the next forward
Like a thread from an unending ball of yarn.

To One

The Spirit with the force of love
Wraps its light around the pair
The central focus in the wedding play
That folks have come from miles to see.
The much-loved son steps on the stage
Where two begin to sing as one
In a life-long drama cast by God,
Where chance would not suffice.
The bride has reached across
To show the way,
But finds the bridegroom standing as a man—
Yet not alone, but arm-in-arm
Where angels sing in chorus from the "Book of Life"
Of days of joy,
Where harmony is soft and warm like eider down;
Of nights that call to stoke the fire anew,
Lest morning comes with chill and clouds
Where dreams once grew.
The sacrament is here laid out,
The symbols for a greater plan,
An act of faith and love and hope
To raise the consciousness of each
To things beyond themselves.
Now, they themselves—
Bright sparks from God,
True souls along a journey
Coming to the central star—the Sun,
The body and the blood become as one,
The Universal One.

Morning of Love

A quiet move—a loving touch.
The languor of sleep still upon us.
Gentle caresses—slow exploration.
No expectations—just giving—
Softness and touch, light as a butterfly's wings.
The feeling of sharing . . .
Nothing taken, nothing given—just sharing.
Easy awareness, almost as if her touch is my touch
And my touch is her touch.
Joint touch . . . joint need . . . soft, soft love.
Fields of touch like velvet skin—her skin, my skin.
No urgency, but growing hunger.
The velvet of hand and lip and response, as all are one;
And, with gentle, yet compelling, release we are one.
Each knows the blessed satisfaction of the other:
The mountain summit to slow climb down—
Savoring the memory of hilltop and present withdrawal as one.
"He maketh me to lie down in green pastures;
He leadeth me beside the still waters."
"He anointeth my head with oil; my cup runneth over"
"He restoreth my soul."
Amen.

Birth

What measures can be applied to our emotions—
It is difficult for the human mind to contemplate—
The subject is so awesome by its nature
When God and Man co-create?
Speak of it in any way you choose:
"Creation," "evolution," "birth,"
It defies the term you use,
As one is entering into Earth.
A matured egg is placed in play
And sperm goes hunting in a certain way;
This one misses and this one hits
And starts a chain of little bits.
A single impregnated egg
Produces fins before a leg
Like it is led
From single cell, to fish with fin
To a taily little amphibian,
Then finally, to a biped
With little legs and big head—
A nine-month documentary
Of a billion years in creation.
Hear me! Hear me now.
We two have set upon the stage our own play
That has had a run of millions of years with one Director.
The script is set but the actors change;
Time and again it is a crowd pleaser—
Fresh to new audiences,
With a few ad-libs thrown in.
In the vernacular of the theatre
This is a replay of a "classic."
And here are we, so newly wed,
With our love, awaiting this one course of nature

That assures our co-creation and procreation.
I say, "I love you!"
She says, "I love you too!"
So soon, so quick, so long the dawning.
Thus, draws the play along.
The happy voice: "I think we did it!"
The pregnant pause: What will this mean?
The long wait of nine months
While learning lines and at rehearsals.
And backstage, concern; must she bear this load alone?
From a small flutter, to tremors slight
To a mighty kick in the night!
After many little quakes and aftershocks,
When the time is right, the trumpet sounds;
The dam breaks;
The plot unwinds as the full moon rises.
The waters pour forth upon the earth
And new life is close behind.
The climactic scene begins.
Bags are packed for fast departing;
She is ready,
I am giddy—starting.
It's a "hurry-up and wait" delivery—
Knowing that the real show's coming.
Her choice is natural birth;
I'm the anesthetic—without training—
But pain is real—what's bravery worth-
Fertile soil without the raining?
She breathes and waits and breathes;
I hold her hand and squeeze and squeeze.
I sit with her throughout the night—
The full moon high.

Contractions ebb and build like savage tides,
While Dr. Moon (yes, Dr. Moon)
Delivers babies in waves—one by one;
Five come to shore that night.
Moon rises from his cot for each presenting—
Bringing babies into Light.
And I was there, like the male wolf scenting,
Waiting and watching to protect my mate—
The nurses uneasy with my descending,
Fearing that I might faint.
(But I am persistent all the same
Since I've got skin in this game.)
Dr. Moon is calm and patient
Accepting her wish to have me present.
Thus begins the final Act.
All must scrub and mask to enter—
After this, no turning back—
Into the white and holy center
Whence new life comes.
I proceed behind the gurney
To provide comfort to my wife
And looking to the end of journey
Where the prize is worth the price.
For her final sacrifice, at last,
She lies as on an altar
(Husbands barred here in the past)
And I stand with my own saltire
To share this holy rite of birth.
Though she does the heavy lifting,
I join to honor and confirm
Her incomparable great gifting
(We all have lessons here to learn).

Dr. Moon urges to push harder;
She wants the pain to be through.
I cajoled, "We're getting closer."
While our excitement grew.
"Here it comes!" Out comes the head.
Suddenly, the room is shining
Like a sky after storm;
My temperature is rising,
Goose bumps are on my arm.
Electric waves keep pulsing,
A new actor comes on stage!
Emerging as an "unveiling"
Of our co-creation with our God—
(Big head, scrawny legs,
Like a crawfish, kicking)
But to me, a wondrous sight.
Choirs of angels begin singing:
"Halleluiah!" on this night.
As, in my head, a voice proclaims:
"This is my son, with whom I am well pleased."
Most magical moment . . . fruition!
All digits, limbs—all sound.
And the newborn—like Tarzan—
Yells a primeval cry of triumph!
A strong rush of love fills me;
I kiss The Mighty Woman Deliverer
Of the Mystery of Life.
Ontogeny recapitulates Phylogeny,
From single cell to Man.
But, no accident this;
The Great Mind has put before us—
(Who shared this creation drama)—

A certainty beyond certainty;
And twice we shared, and know
That this is more than a physical occurrence.
Whatever biochemistry had gone before,
Whatever physical aspects,
There is something more–
The Creation of Man!

Can I Describe The Joy You Are To Me?

Can I describe the joy you are to me?
A stream of pleasure rushing to a hungry sea—
A warming sun upon a snowy hill
Where a yearning soul can come to take its fill.
You cannot speak except you turn me on;
Your "No" is better than most "Yeses" I have known.
Your "Yes" is but the first note to a song
That sweetens more intensely as it goes along.

A Close Relation

She brightens my morning;
She warms my night.
Her friendship is my sustaining air—
My energy source that lights the way.
With her beside me I am ready to face the world.
When she is sick, I hurt;
When we are crossed, the air is heavy and tense.
Her pain is my pain; her joy is my joy.
She is my love, my friend, my wife.

A Flower Grows

A flower grows on the mountain;
It grows for me.
It grows out of my lonely niches
And in my light and bright corners.
Its tendrils are curled around my heart.
I call it "Norma."

Closeness

Love is a landscape—
The hills are green and lovely from afar,
The rocks do not show.
Neither does the distant view reveal the intimate flowers,
The scent of moss and fern, the chirping birds,
Nor the sweet companion who makes sleeping and waking
    worthwhile.
Each morning when I hear the first pull of drawer or click of
    step
Meaning and purpose are refreshed by closeness and detail.

Where Is the Beauty of My Love?

Where is the beauty of my love—
In the hard red clay?
Where is the beauty of my love—
In tears for loss?
My selfish cry for loss—
The empty spaces; objects passed?
Where was the beauty of my love
Before that day I creamed her tea?
So young, so fresh, such piquancy—
The memories of a burning love?
The ache—tears, aches, tears . . .
Where is touch? Where is taste?
And sight and sound—
Days and nights—and years?
Where is the beauty of my love?

The Train

Oh mewling train don't come to me with your lonesome cries;
You bring to me the memories of my love now gone.
(She loved the train as nostalgia from her past)
You trains are destined to move on; you will not last.
So take away your mournful clickity-clack;
Your chatter will not bring her back.
 It is a fact: Your voice grows dim.
Your distant sound leaves me behind.

My Rose of Sharon

"I am a rose of Sharon,
A lily of the valley." *
White blossomed beauty—
Courageous against the hurricanes of life—
Leaning from the winds of Fran,
Still blooms with magnificent profusion.
(Nature is a giver of great gifts
That we often overlook
Or take too lightly.)
A flowering bush or fruiting tree
Provide "fruits of the spirit"
Beyond "our daily bread."
A woman whose daily gifts of softness,
Welcome sights and sounds—
Sweet scents;
Lives in memory as nature's gift to me.

(* Song of Solomon 2:1)

My Heart

First, a sense of harmony that quietly melds
And builds like Spring grows into Summer sun.
A rush that does not fade away—
It speaks to body, mind, and more—
Like liberty's spread arms that open wide the door.
Out of the tempest also comes the calm—
The reassuring peace, like a compass rests on point;
A point that shows the way where travelers seek
       to end the day, and find their ease.
Much unknown here; much left to faith;
But still, that early harmony pervades the air—
No difference will cause imbalance to prevail.
Where weeds grow, flowers will grow as well.
It truly is an exciting time—an agelessness
       that lifts beyond the prime.
What fresh renewal awaits the two of us—
       alive with struggle and with bliss?
We'll kiss each day the risky hem of this;
And, upon each discovery that we seize,
We'll savor more the pleasures of the eve.

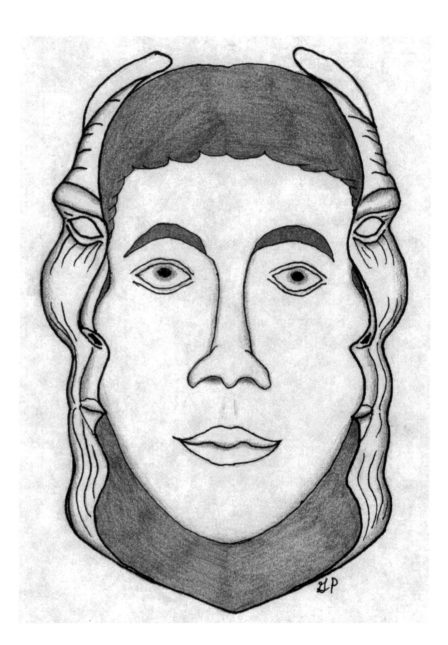

The Child Within

I bought a sculpture at the show—
A face within a face.
It struck me as a place I'd been
And a path that I must trace.
The outer mien—the older one—
Is the face that most will see;
The inner face is the face I know—
The face I see as me.
The child within whose skin is smooth,
Whose hair is brown, not gray,
Who's full of sparkle and of life,
Will come "right out" and play.
The clothes I wear will come and go—
I'll trade them in when worn—
They really are a passing thing,
Not covering me when born.
The me that's me is light as air,
A steady breeze, a day that's fair,
That doesn't age or need repair.
The body changes—age takes its toll,
But has little effect upon the soul.

La Belle

Indeed, you are "La Belle,"
But, what indeed are you?
You make me ache
And anguish, it is true;
The wind is hot and makes me sweat;
It's cold and turns me chill.
I look from off a viewing stand
While grappling with my will.
It seems you open everything,
But is everything too much;
Is open, open or open closed?
Is it a boundless sea
With ancient monsters lurking there,
To take a bite of me?
I do not fear a bite or two,
But will I surely drown;
Will I suffocate beneath
The roaring, smashing sound?
In what dimension do man and woman meet?
In what restaurant do they eat?
Is there a man's chair and a woman's seat?
Can a man encircle woman
If she encircles more?
"Poor Sisyphus doomed to tumble and toss
The notable stone that gathers no moss."
Is a revolving door a "revolving" door
Or just a door?
If I approach it as a door,
Is it no more?
If I swim in the sea will it buoy me?
If the wind blows hot or cold,

Won't I fly?
Will you join me wing to wing
And not look back—
Or drift away to a bluer sky—
And wonder why?
Even when the winds are strong
My wings can protect you there
Until the sky is fair.
And, in the calmness of the tree
We can cuddle, you and I,
And dream of little treats we share;
Just peace and tenderness—
No tenseness in the air.
Please, do not bite me La Belle,
Or, if you do, please kiss it well.

My Thoughts are Singing

We have bonded, you and I;
We have tripped the light fantastic—
Poured it out before the other—
Opened wide the door and further.
We have poked the hidden places
To make the ravens fly.
We have discovered secret treasures—
Diamonds, art and writings;
Emptied memories to the barest skins;
Discussed childhood, middle and old, ages—
Weaknesses, strengths and tests we'd meet;
Sleeping habits, spontaneous pleasures
And the various foods we'd eat.
When you're young, time isn't measured.
When you're older—grayer, fatter—
Wiser, more experienced, sadder,
Then each must move his/her own ladder
To this place that now must matter;
Each rung bears the steps and miss-steps
That will act as pre-preps—
Frightening as these are,
And passing at the speed of light.
Will they take us into sunshine
Or to some other darker night?
I have pondered on these things.
We have asked so many questions
But in my heart I know the answers.
Arm in arm, we know the answers;
Hand in hand, we make the future—
Each and each the other's teacher.
My whole heart is here to serve you

But your light will not require it;
Your whole heart is set to serve me—
I receive that that serves you only:
Corresponding mutual—
Mutual love respecting self and other.
What I have, I offer freely;
Time is fleeting, fleeting, fleeting.
Let us meet now in the center.

Bright Is Our Star

The magnitude and magnificence of your presence
Puts me in a reverential state.
What will the length, breadth and depth
Of this relationship be?
Like a jungle safari—what will we find?
Wild animals hid among the trees?
What crystal pools of bliss await, as well?
This will not be for the faint of heart—
A hunger so powerful that a one-year wait
Seems like the vastness of the Milky Way.
I want you Now!
We have shared our experiences—
(Almost too graphically)—
To permit a full and honest view;
But, even so, the heat that forged the past
Will continue to fire the furnace
Which will grow and build our future.
With our years has come much knowledge;
Can we now act with shared-wisdom
(As wisdom is knowledge used aright)?
I pledge to you my honest, earnest and loving effort
To forge our joint purposes upon
The wisdom of the Christ spirit;
That, hand in hand, we may kneel together,
Pray together, and meditate together;
That I will share with you in service to our neighbors;
And, in that same deep spirit of love and consideration,
I will honor your body, mind and spirit
And seek with you the daily feast
Of joy in all we do.

Union

Shall we be joined—
We are two flames so hot to touch?
(Is a small fire enough to cook the meal?)
Two flames so hot they will combust (burn up)!
Must we set backfires lest the forest burns entire?
Can we only touch—surely that's not too much.
But "too much" is not enough!
I think it is okay; just let it burn—exhaust itself, burn out.
No! No! Eternal flame—amour eternal!
From embers of first love she gets her glow then bursts forth again.
Contrary to the view of some, a fire is good
                              for the forest now and then.
The old trees are gone but new life will begin.
In the circle of my arms, new life begins.
In the circle of her arms the fires restart.
If this eternal joining brings us Spring
It surely is a holy thing.

Just Supposing Juxtaposing

Together—juxtaposed—
Like two eyes and a nose;
As two bees upon a rose
Extracting honey as it flows;
We are a pair of one
Like the moon reflecting sun.
Soon we'll be one in skin—
And what will we do then?
Will we become the next of kin?
And isn't that a sin?
You may be excused
If you refused,
Or ask to be recused.
If you are tired of juxtaposing
You may change your juxtaposition.
It may help you at your leisure,
Infusing you with pleasure;
And isn't that the measure
That shows the success of juxtaposing?

This Is A Poem

You are the earth woman filled with the lust for life;
Running over with sexuality—wrestling with the world,
Pulsing powerful energy.
I struggle, I straddle, I surrender—
The weight of the earth upon me.
I smell the earth in my face;
Breath leaves my lungs.
My body becomes stiff—encased in earth.
The earth overlaps and overcomes.
In conquest the earth lies still.
Resurrection!
The earth opens.
I rise again.
All things spring back to life.
The cycle of life continues.

The Dance

We dance the dance—
The sexual dance of mating;
We proclaim our status boldly—
Pushing it forward to announce
Our readiness for the ancient rite.
The male moves forward;
The female moves forward, then back.
She turns away as if uninterested.
The male moves forward;
The female moves forward, then aside—
Seeming to listen for other sounds.
She moves forward again.
He pushes forward; she runs around.
He stands still—befuddled.
He shakes his head to clear the fog.
She tiptoes forward;
He moves slowly forward.
They touch; they mate.
Together, sound and fury!
Then, she goes back to the herd.
He stares—perplexed.
Finally, they pursue their normal ways.
She seeks his comfort in time of crisis;
He seeks her presence in time of need.
The ancient ritual resolves into civilized behavior—
A unit for comfort and protection,
And to preserve the ancient ways.
But a new dance begins.
Within the boundary of a room
A muted rhythm can be felt.
How civilized are we?

Should we be guided by
Our gender mysteries—
Domesticated mammals
Within a ritual dance?
Or, drawn together
As the completion of
A painting which runs free,
Forming a picture for
The eyes and mind and heart;
That, though now, One,
Still continues to transform
Within the frame of life.

SECTION III

Awareness

In a nothingness so deep, so dark, so vast ....
The Great Mind was still .... silent ....
. . . .

What was that?
I don't know. I didn't hear anything. I didn't see anything.
I know, but I sensed something.
How could you have sensed something? I didn't feel anything.
I don't know; but there is something. Listen .... Be still.
Are you sure? I don't hear anything.
Be still!
I don't hear anything but you.
Yes!
Now I hear it. It sounds like you.
Be still! ....
How can I know with you here—talking? Remove yourself.
Now I sense it ....
But maybe it's me ....
Do I sense myself? ....
Is it "other?" ....
. . . .
Where did you go? Come back! ....
. . . .
Come back! I'm lonely! ....
Oh, there you are. Good! I need you. Where did you go?
I was here.
But, I couldn't see you.
I know.
Why couldn't I see you?
You shut me out.
Well, yes, but not really. I'm glad you're here.
Where did you go?
You sent me away.

Where?

Out of your mind.

But, where?

Everywhere.

But I wanted to know where you were.

I am here.

Will you stay here?

If you want me to.

I need a companion.

I am your companion.

I need someone whom I can depend on.

I am that someone.

But, you left me alone.

No. You shut me from your mind.

At that moment but . . .

You can't have it both ways. You either want me here or not.

Yes. I do want you here . . . .

Then I am here.

The Stolen Pearls

Wallow no longer in your own self-righteousness—
Swine before which Christ would not cast down his pearls;
But they have stolen them, broken into the treasury of God
And come out wearing Christ's raiment
Shouting, "I Am that I Am!"
The thief has set the tune to sing by:
"There is none that understandeth;
there is none that seeketh after God."
But he does.
He says, "I will show you what you must do to be saved.
Believe in me. Christ expounded the way,
But if Christ contradicts me, follow what I say.
I wear Christ's robe (*the stolen cloak*);
I see you choose to think for yourself and believe what Jesus spoke.
You are evil!
I have shown you the way of eternal life: Except ye believe
     in me . . .
You are evil; you choose to reason.
Christ would not cast his riches before me so I have seized it;
Thereby, I thrust the beam from mine eye.
I have the pearls of judgment!
Except you believe in me . . .
You are evil; you choose to reason."
In whom shall I believe—Christ or his pretender?
And who is Christ and who Pretender?
And who the serpent?
I am that I am. The swine have stolen the pearls.

Timeless

We make too much of "time."
"Time" is important in this plane only
Where we expend our days in blocks
By watching calendars and clocks:
"Is this your period?"
"When is your baby due?"
"It's time to feed the baby!"
"Hurry, the school bus is here!"
"When will Dad be home?"
Ah-h, just relax—unfold
"In patience you possess your soul."
Recognize, with good intention,
That your soul has no dimension.
Let's begin at the beginning,
In a ball game without inning,
(Without the benefit of mud or rib bone)
You and I as sparks from God,
Not some elemental sod,
But more the energy from Sun,
Became a part of eternal One.
Time is material in the Earth,
As we progress from birth to birth
From devolution to evolution,
But time is not relevant to our souls.
We are not the least infernal;
Rather, are we lives eternal.
Yet life to life in many sessions
Here to learn our various lessons—
Attracted, not just incidental,
To those most instrumental.
(You may have been my mother
And I your son or lover.)

Thus, we come together—
It isn't "Why" or "Whether"—
To celebrate our perfecting,
(Or to rectify imperfecting),
Along a timeless run
Back to the One.

Focus

Energy needs a resting place
But that place attracts its own—
None other than the place that it needs most
Will call it forth.
Energy, focused, becomes light
When brought to bear at a certain point.
Energy, dispersed, is wasted water
Spreading out across an empty space,
Coursing as gravity leads—
Nowhere for sure;
A useful force when brought together as the river,
Each drop contained within the whole;
The energizer and the energized
Become one point of light
Lifting each other like a flood.

The Observer

I sit upon a high hill and look down upon myself
Sometimes I am one and then the other—
And sometimes both at the same time.
I look near and I look far;
I see selfishness—I see better acts
And I see pride in those acts.
I see little perfection but no great evil either.
Omissions galore—at six, at sixteen, at twenty-six.
I ask the Other, "Why—why is this?"
"Why do I stand by and watch
As others degrade my brothers—
And do nothing?"
Small acts—too small to count?
How I weep inside!
Can I wash away my feeling
That I failed my brother?
Too young—powerless (excuses)?
A coward? Was I a coward?
It hangs upon my soul.
Can I truly see myself?
Can I judge myself?
The albatross hangs heavy around my neck;
When I weigh in, its toe is on the scales.
Can I free myself by weeping now?
Will the heavy bird drop off?
Must I atone—atone—atone?
Alone? Alone? Alone?
"As you did it to the least of these, my brothers,
You did it unto me."
Oh, Observer of my soul
When will I be free?

The Talk Show

We bring you all the news . . .
Huh . . . huh?
Up in the polls; down in the polls.
Political speak: We are working for you.
Is that true?
Reality check: What the heck?
Get real. How much can he steal?
Who's the boss? Whitewater froth.
Tumble and toss—tumble and toss.
Can't be bold. Tent's gonna fold. Put it on hold,
Airwave fluff—Beautiful actress in *Bombshell*.
All the news. Can we choose?
Talkity-talk; berate, berate.
We are great! How do we rate?
Hunger in Rwanda. Ohh . . . ooh.
What'll we do?
Blowout is box office hit!
Elements right. Bloody fight. Sex at night.
Have you seen it, Katie?
Bosnian Serbs shell Sarajevo. Ho . . . hum.
Don't be glum.
New diet fills your needs.
Poppy seeds.
Have you tried it, Katie?
No exercise. That's great!
Weighty-weight.
Football star, "mayhem and vent:"
To young peoples' causes gives one percent;
Love him, love him; pays his rent.
Uh oh. What's that?
Hits his wife with a baseball bat.
He shouldn't do that.

Hero, hero. Oh . . . oh.
Excuse the fact; was a passionate act.
Bryant, refugees die; children cry.
U.S. to pay. It will go away.
Katie, have you seen the new fashion?
See-through is you. Above the thigh.
Legs are bare. Don't stare.
Show and tell. Well-well.
Crimes shoot high. No one knows why.
It's a shame; who's to blame?
Barbie riding the crest, tall and thin.
Fourteen year old anorexic died yesterday.
Too fat to play, her coaches say.
Do you still have your Barbie, Katie?
Mental illness, nervous decay . . .
Have you had one, Katie?
What does your psychiatrist say?
Get away? Well . . . well.
You need a second home, a place to go.
Welfare moms charged with fraud.
Tsk . . . tsk; laudy . . . laud.
Latchkey kids . . . Childcare woes . . . Uh . . . oh.
Shakespeare in a jiffy. Jots and tittle.
It helps to know just a little.
Middle East Jihad . . . bomb squad . . .
Many dead. Filled with lead.
Dissent is good. Should, would, could.
Really did.
Western fires burning bright.
Firefighters die. Fight, fight, fight.
Watch the sky. My . . . my.
Fibercom or Metamucil, I can't tell.

Congested highways—bridges fell.
Have you ever golfed in Yakima, Bryant?
A mile wide, an inch deep—
Time to talk; no time to think.
Shrink, shrink, shrinkity-shrink—
Don't feel; don't blink. Run it by fast, you miss the link.

To A Young Woman On Graduation From College

Congratulations are not due; the struggle is before.
And though I'm just ahead of you, I have seen the sight in store.
Therefore, I know the animals—I have seen them through the
    trees.
The Hydra and the Cyclops were not more terrible than these.
Conformity, Mediocrity, and the Greed Of Men—
Only praise yourself for learning what these are
For these will be your enemies or friends;
These will crush you constantly to par.
Become the protégé of Prudence—ogle her at first;
Explain to her the magnitude and rightness of your thirst.
Tell her that a friend of yours is traveling with the beasts;
Has seen their hungry, grinning faces;
Has seen them cudgel with their maces
The willy-nilly and the weak for feasts.
Win the lady to your side by praising her great eyes—
Her feminine heart will be moved by your tries.
Then let her glimpse your unprotected innocence and virtue—
Her soul will weep and shatter her with sighs.
She'll grant you vision to see, with a fence protecting you,
What the man-eating beasts have done and can do.
Don't stand too close! Watch from this safe place;
Remember the hypnotic powers of the serpent and cover your
    face.
Surprised to see the city on the screen?
That's not a city; it's an academy
Where all the people dress alike,
And act alike, and talk alike—
And mirror without thinking.
Has evolution developed some new kind?
No—animals still—man has no mind.
There are the freaks—these are mutations;

They have a will, but are in such small portion.
Can I recall those in that class?
No need; you know them all—
Just look above the mass—
Those foolish great men whose thoughts were new frontiers;
But they were unique, not entombed at birth by fears
That thinking alerts Man to the wretched animal "Compromise"
Which credits his wit so little, it wears no disguise.
"But the moving mass, like oxen at the wheel,"
You say, "We're not ambitious.
It did not seek diploma as a ticket for a meal."
Look closely: They are all together in the stew-pot of the town;
Graduates and laborers all taste the same and wear one gown.
The gold standard is the standard standard
So, like a male grouse before his fiancée,
Men preen themselves in costumes of the day.
Their repertoire of trite, unfeeling words
Spring up in conversation as startled birds.
Those superficial things, which are called good,
However little liked or understood,
Are praised by the invertebrates as though
It is the test to discover what they know.
But here is breathed the breath that makes one cry:
They will not tolerate the honest doubt;
Instead, they cultivate dishonest lie.
Don't smile and say you know the kind I mean . . .
I speak of those like you who play at games that have no sting—
Cum lauds who rose above their lazy brothers,
The leaders of so many unimportant things, and all the others,
Who will be cast into a world that doesn't foster the cut of
    truth—
The illumination of the foibles of the ruling class,

The willy-nilly mass.
We'll meet the ambitious one ten years hence.
Stay back from the fence!
The man dressed formally in a uniform suit,
Planning his stratagem to get more gold,
Was once a seeker after Truth
Whose naïve mind has not foretold
The real beasts that exist.
He left the school as much a fool as he had entered it
Since he had not seen, as you now see,
The always-present monsters.
Five years he slept and also dreamed;
But then he ceased to dream.
Somniferous beast, suspected least,
Had grogged him with its eye!
His citadel crushed by the fierce thrust—
A man began to die.
Then cupid's dart pierced the heart of the dying man;
So shorn of reason and lashed by love
He was wed in hateful haste.
This prolific Pandora that the dying man sought
Increased the burdens that the other beasts wrought
Permitting the last beast to devour
The last living morsel of man.
Greedy GREEDOMEN, with infinite claws,
Closes his ghastly cavernous jaws—
And snaps the spine of dying ambition.
Drag the carcass to the pasture.
"How fine, how fine to be interred
With all with whom the world was shared—"
Of willy-nilly nature.
Thus the monsters of the earth may chide

And seek to make of you their bride;
But prove yourself of Herculean line
And to the labyrinth of Man give new design.

Split Pea

"Oh, that is wonderfully esoteric. It speaks of the earth and everything."

"It is sacrilegious and filthy. It's pure 'crotch' art."

"The artist was angry. He must be allowed to speak his piece."

"I am a citizen and my peace is disturbed."

"But she was molested and raped. She simply expresses her metamorphosis.

Why, the snakeskin clearly shows that."

"But what about the glove between her legs dripping some dark iridescent fluid?

I am confused by the loud, shrilly voices. Where is the line?

Nobody answers the questions: What about me? What about my right to choose?"

"You can choose to look or not."

"But I choose that it not be in a public gallery."

"That is censorship!"

"But what about my right to choose?"

"Well, you have to compromise."

"But what about you. I feel like an infinitesimal pea on the floor being stomped by shiny black boots and I am being accused of wearing them."

"A pea is just a pea; art is A-R-T."

"Life is full of self-regulation. Why must I be eaten without a 'Thank you?'

My tennis shoes are white. Where is my Calhoun?"

"Ignorance cannot excuse you for being in the majority.

Don't turn the other cheek to me! I want to push it in your face."

"Why? Don't I have a right?"

"You have a right to accept my excesses;

To surrender to my rights to be vulgar

And to force my interpretation of 'art' on you.

Accept it or I will scream: First amendment! Discrimination! Censorship!

If you have the balls, you too can be disgusting—You pea."

The Caws

The Ashe House crows congregate
Like shouters at Speakers' Corner.
They must relate
Their angry messages of hate:
"Fight for the cause!
Caw—caw—caw!"
Will I observe,
Will I look back
On bloody deeds
And see their track
Of martyrdom foretold?
Black Jack leads the pack;
With the biggest voice
He cuts no slack.
He sends his fanatic followers out
To foment fear.
What trickery is this?
Does Black Jack know
Where all his terrorists go?
"Catch him ... catch him by the tail;
This way you'll break his spell!"
Yet Jack himself does not know
Where all his messages go.
Spun off by hate ... or ... what?
Black Jack is here—or not?
All citizens must stay awake—
They must not sleep—
For fear the unknown terrors
From the darkness creep.
Can any push it back,
Even Jack?
He cast his track;

He can't get it back.
What religion does he sell
That takes his followers to hell—
Where Black Jack lives?
Jack himself will not go there
While martyrdom is in the air.
The message that the Crowists spew is:
"Do as I say, not as I do."
How long, how far, can Black Jack talk
While innocents die and his young stalk?
As thoughts are deeds across the world,
What thoughts will counter these?
"If all good people stayed at home . . . ?"
"If all took up the fight . . . ?"
"If all would face the darkness down . . .
Would they come again tonight?"
Is this the view that Crowists see?
Is this their weaponry?
If all the rest stay home
And let the Crowists fly
And bomb 'til all do die . . .
If all that's left is death
And terror on the fly
(All at the Crowists' will)
What will the Crowists then?
Who has the last caw?
Who can crow; and who eats crow?
And when the crows are gone,
Does the blue bird sing?

Katrina Forecast

Who could know how the wind would blow,
How the seas would turn upside down—
And water would cover the ground;
That thirty-foot waves would crash into shore
And houses would be no more;
Lifelong memories would be covered by dirt—
And the hurt . . . and the hurt . . . and the hurt?

(On returning from Bay St. Louis, Mississippi)

Poor Pluto

I think that I will never know
A planet like little Pluto—
A planet invisible to the naked eyes,
Three billion miles across the skies.
But in God's wisdom, as things are,
Scientists decreed it now sub-par.
Astrologers are all in tears
As dwarfing Pluto feeds their fears
That diminishing Venus may come next
And love will end without pretext.

ABOUT THE AUTHOR

"Who am I?" Today I become naked before any who choose to read this book. How worthy does any person in this situation feel?

My journey in poetry has been life-long. At an early age I was a close observer of the things around me. Fond impressions of nature, sights, smells, and the sounds on our family farm and family trips still rise up in my memory—today, fresh as then; even darker memories of the dimly lighted kitchen where my grandfather's body was laid out for the "wake"—the smell of kerosene lamps and the heavy feeling of sadness. I was three or four.

Books in a small bookcase in my parents' home drew me to nursery rhymes and, especially, Longfellow's *Song of Hiawatha*.

I wrote a play in the third grade for my class to perform. It was hardly an august beginning. The play had no ending.

I began writing poetry in high school, trying to express those earlier thoughts and sensations. Something was speaking inside of me that wanted to get out. That same thing keeps me writing poetry today. It seemed like such a personal thing, but after doing some poetry readings where a surprising number of people came and expressed words of interest and actually showed by their comments that they related my poems to things in their own lives—they wanted copies of my poems. From this I saw that I needed to have my poems published.

The Phoenix Collection and Other Poems covers a variety of subjects: nature, the life cycle i.e. love, marriage, birth, death and aging, and some more mystical and spiritual areas. I will be complimented if some of these touch the readers and their lives in some way.

—MAX PRESTON